The Upstairs Room

Dave Buracker

The Upstairs Room

Copyright © 2018 by Dave Buracker

All rights reserved. No part of this book may be reproduced or transmitted in any form or by any means without written permission of the author.

Cover painting: "When You Told Me" by Dave Buracker (2016)
24"x24" - acrylic, paste, gel, spray paint, marker on canvas

Cover design by Jo Dominguez

Library of Congress Control Number: 2018936901

ISBN: 978-0-9915772-9-3

Published by Shabda Press
Pasadena, CA 91107
www.shabdapress.com

The Upstairs Room is a collection of work generated between 2012-2016. Special thanks to Shabda Press and Teresa Mei Chuc in appreciating and recognizing this work. Also, thanks (in no particular order) to the following: Tracy Buracker, Angela Marie Carter, Paul, Cara and Bradley Walton, my family, Pat and Marty Machowsky, Jim Nipe, and Sarah Elizabeth Murphy.

Dave Buracker
November 2016

Contents

How To Fade..1
Pale..2
Swarm...3
What Joseph Said...4
Seven Corners...5
Figments..6
Flwrs..7
Dig You Up..8
Cartography...9
Now Mother...11
Flim Flam..12
The Upstairs Room...13
So We Are Dead...14
Salt of Shore..15
American Alchemy..16
Convinced..18
The Charnel House...19
Postmortem Mockingbird....................................20
Wearing Masks..21
Faint As Starlight..22
A Palm Reader..24
Altar...25
Warsaw...26
Tunnel...27
Dry...29
How It Ends..30
Peeling..33
Drown..34
Geography in Ether...35
Full of Noise..36

Wake	37
Five	38
Wake the Goddess	40
Land of the Blind	41
Train Stop	43
Some Kind of Mass	44
Tasks	46
Painted Saints	47
Stage Two	48
Fear of Gold	50
Sickle Moon	51
District	52
Paint the Stars	53
Sleeping Alone	55
Rewind	56
The Groundskeepers	57
The Wick	58
Concussion	59
Stowaway	60
Shivering	61
Tolls	62
Dry	63
Everything is Just Fine	64
The Fog	65
Cult of Self	66
For Lovers	67
Anthems (for a Generation)	69
Resort Photograph	70
Monster	71
Torchlight	72
You in Delphi	73

How To Fade

Three days ago, the red fox
on the highway was stilled,

almost to mantle of kudzu
grappling still life gravel sliced.

Two days ago, the red fox
on the highway opened,

tail splintered orange shards
on fresh ice refracting ornate.

One day ago, the red fox
on the highway faded,

revealing how to disappear
from a missed leap.

Pale

The ruin value of pale
pulls crow feet with
freckled crowns in
elegant decay;

hands are columns,
stone cracked with
native conquests in
carnage memory.

A patina of blood
oxidizes dreams in
faded copper symmetry,
imperfect sleep –

washes upon the shore

dissolves.

Swarm

Gravel in my shoe
under the overpass
of granite rose petals

could not cut as a
monolith ghost gyre of
exhaust carving clouds,

could not pollinate
street lamp pistils,
exfoliate plastics.

At night, store-front
facades call concrete
pillars to prayer -

excommunicated
under electric light,
locusts swarm.

What Joseph Said

A pre-disposition to play hero,
hard-wired as action star,
activated by archetype;

thrashing wooden swords
towards threshold guardian tower,
trash before treasure.

In the backyard oak shadow,
a child's fear creeps to
windows at night.

Perhaps our caste is coded
with dream memory DNA,
held in double helix,

a triple play solitary line
piercing protein spiral
sequence, pronounces.

Through tireless campaigns
before curtains fall, we cut
- to shed the dark.

Seven Corners

Pawn shop pornography
and mosque collide on

pavement - the great
artery of Washington.

There is a strange geometry
of a seven corner gang sign

on silk road rental stores -
before banners and burqas.

Under traffic light crucible,
a dance of vagrants and

noodle shop vagabonds
blind blood lines, pulse.

Hispanic botanical Santeria
store revels tight tight with

dames jean day laborers
east of eden center jettison

quinceanera candles waltz
waltz ribbons on route fifty

west, awash in the wake
of German sedans.

Figments

Unwind droplights, untangle
twine of dithered doll strings.

A Roman draft proposal, dead
draft of parchment – a design

for another fall from tin tacks,
a figment to quell quarters.

I would like to order a golden
calf, a flank of compassion;

howling lupine Buddha breath
lunitidal, spitting flame sutra.

We need apparitions to be real,
a neon Nazarene by candlelight.

Flwrs

Flags are always half-mast
in my Fatherland, half-lit
past parking lot lamps
through foliage.

Super marts simplify death,
dervish of digital rage - a
sugar dirge sweetens
the swan song.

Mother loses magic when
iris searches engines,
cradles fall near dark,
flowers mean nothing.

They are just
flowers
<flwrs>
</f>

Dig You Up

Expelled forth in dark
from glandular planets,
a sudden race to climb.

A race for relevance, push
through surface to seed -
conception is the first heat.

We are bred to breathe
from womb to waltz past
wagons in the slow lane;

fiberglass shells winding
up fallopian exit ramps
to penetrate stars.

This is why we love
a second coming,
or a sequel.

So I will dig you up.
So you must go.
So you cannot sleep.

Cartography

Crammed into coastal concrete hives,
we fear billboard broadcasts behind
retinas, reminding us of late

night paid programming orphans,
that cancer is coming and some
side effects may occur.

Pacified into documenting dead stars,
we wear death mask dunce caps,
in an instant land where we forget –

so we burn our camera catalogs;
we were here, in a travesty of trysts,
loved by strangers, like you lust you,

probability engines chart next leaps
as automatic cartographer because
we trust everything spilled,

    dissected -
here comes the choo choo.

Here comes the death cult mocking,
the fine, fair fin de siècle, corpse-pale
adolescence framed in filters, a cinematic

    requiem reposted -
this is animism with animation.

"We are already dead," said the
news column, a simulation calculated,
a glitch in mathematics.

We are already dead from
monogamy and monotony,
the Christ coloring books

washed in monochrome,
and unfiltered apathy drugs
excreted into water;

we hide in polaroid youth,
we do not live for tomorrow,
we can only catalog today

- we are already dead.

Now Mother

The death lust watch
of man has devoured
forests in greed,

an atomic detritus of
Adam-poisoned wells,
where spears fell.

Taste blood and body,
waste blood and body;
wafers of flesh to forget –

men have lost
the moon.

This is the time of
woman - to dispel
fear, heal the howl

as now mother
nature is a mother
world is a mother;

we have followed
fathers to their son
and holy ghost

lured to an empty host –

this is the time for woman.

Flim Flam

We lose control as
spectator, spectral
tyranny or tease.

Capacity of knives,
an electric high chair
singing aural affirmation.

I am floating in fluid,
intimations of innocence
erupts nothing.

Your wound interface
numbs boundaries
with fertile flim flam.

Your invisible violations are
perverse engines of
minimal memory.

The Upstairs Room

Construct a blanket fort
in the new model house;

My head is ringing,
a dead telegraph wire.

I stay in the upstairs room
as a fevered school boy;

where I can watch robins
leap upon a patched lawn,

they look for crows on
telephone lines, as I peek

from a dusted panes' mantle,
I can see everyone from

this fugue shadow – waiting for
strangers, waiting for crows.

So We Are Dead

Nothing is truly dust but
dead skin oscillating in

circuit motor fans electric
murmur of machines;

nothing is truly dead but
a drone of recycled air

stirring ten thousand
thread count silks over

pale skin dreaming in
well-carpeted cages;

so now I understand
why people jump to

kiss granite in a
gravity game where

we envy wings and
wish to hurry nature's

flight of feather,
flurry of flesh,

sacrifice memory
sets our motion,

we pollinate silicon,
so we are dead.

Salt of Shore

We are by nature an infection,
wet-wired to wander west,
snuffing native grounds,

forage into frontier, Odysseus,
for salt to preserve wounds
where we buried gods.

We are by nature trappers,
thirsting forest bounties,
dredging fool's gold lust

in desert laments dreaming
junk yard ground jowls,
a mesa mouth metallic.

We are by nature wounded,
without war paint to annex
plains blind to banners beyond

birch wood on the shore,
where foam breaks at dark,
when we drink the sea.

American Alchemy

[I take three pills]

I.

Pills to forget death,
devoured gauze face
signals drifting wireless;

my only sunshine
you are always
excreted first.

Discard and disregard
smudged safety seals
reset button of bottle caps,

we load text in
dead place digital
charnel channels.

II.

Pills to slow a heart rate,
rated for violent content
rated for mature audiences;

every step kicks
dander, dried lover
as dead lotus.

We cannot read stars
through plastic blinds
with plastic sextants.
So we lay supine to
flat screens shuddering
Anglo pixel portents.

III.

A pill to prevent clots,
poison popped
fear of punches;

frail princess propped
on pillows, fear
of razors stilled;

fear of stiletto spills
hemorrhage horror
face fantasy,

where I shatter like
glass - a fun house
mirror.

Convinced

    Today I am convinced
in the Cathar belief
our world belongs to Satan -

who rules below
a night sky.

    Today I am convinced
the consolamentum, the heretical
purification of Cathars before death,

to absolve sin, could be the
origin of catharsis - to purge.

    Today I am convinced
that the medicine, a catharsis,
which induces defecation,

was coined by a Catholic
in disgust of duality.

    Today I am convinced
that if I believed in god,
I would be a Cathar - as

we live in the detritus
of all that is mighty.

The Charnel House

In an adoration of Adonis,
women plant seeds at a
garden gate to blossom

from torn goddess bosom,
burning night blisters,
nectar of stars shimmer

milk in soil wither winter's
impermanence with poppy
tears to illuminate the

charnel house lamentation,
as Chinese lanterns dance
before the storm breaks.

From lilac hours, blood
transmutes black dogs
to mirror sleep,

Through cult reverie
of elegies, a reverence
of youth dance to the river.

Postmortem Mockingbird

When you were alive,
an aloof mockingbird

on mother's chimney top
would chirp all morning.

After you passed, the
bird bounced through

the open basement door,
she beckoned it to leave.

Years later when I visit
the old house, a solitary

mockingbird modulates
its incessant manifesto

all night as a tone poem
to insomnia, under stars;

I hope it sleeps all day,
I hope it always sleeps.

Wearing Masks

Ears are open to
concrete detours,

strangers taste
where I feast alone;

devoured under
sanguine moons,

smells of Mary blood
damsels, innocent

burning banners
toasting tattered

seductions of myself
dancing under shop-lit

walks with animal
mask growls.

There are no sirens -
we are all Jezebel

in first position.

Faint As Starlight

Dear Stranger -

I know you are still there.
You are not breathing but
I feel the cord moving.

We are tethered to each other,
thousands of miles apart,
umbilical under starlight;

sitting in this cold room,
sleepless before dawn,
I feel the space torn from

where you once stood
with your child, where
a bomb fell silently.

The gravity of concrete,
vacuum of your last breath,
choking on blood and dust;

your child's hand fell
in a violent wake, a void
where bitter space begins.

Stranger, you are still here,
at the other end of ether
dangling on this wire;

my eyes weep for you,
strings draw you, pull
you both as ghost forms,

pulling closer to me,
stilled in a dark room -
we are faint as starlight.

A Palm Reader

A palm reader
traced tridents and
tributaries of skin,

under an orange
umbrella of horror
pop stars said…

"Your Father died,
you will be sick and
drawn to the sea."

In the minuscule
marginalia of lines
reaping reprisals,

raging in the heat of
supple swamp light
— she was right.

Altar

Grinding the rind of lust
the rust spark unyielding,
wakes from sleep in a
darkened lake, lapping
slumbered lips parched.

Perverse in my dream
of your spent silk
nestled against skin
-a hidden altar.

I am a thunderstorm
winding on peaks,
an offering upon
your skin.

Warsaw

City of the Dead;
your east block facades

plastered over burnt brick
are covered with telecom

billboards snuffing Roma
flower girls and ghettos.

Past Krasinskich Square
candles in glass stand

in corners at night,
still lit in rain where

they huddled in rain
and were killed -

grandchildren
remember.

I bought a tin Teutonic
charm in old town -

protection from an
untimely death.

Tunnel

I.

Boxcars squeal to breadlines,
in vagabond concrete sleep;
tap dance on ticker tape, a
medal-wound morphine march,

rusted rivet tongues lash at
silver screen Kaisers in
automatic sky writing with
carbine fingers.

And Orpheus fox trots feral,
through opiate smoke waving
whiskey bottles empty as an
iron lung on Broadway.

Rail lines leave neon clouds
for red lanterns on nights
where bells ring under stars.

We are children at the train stop
waiting for native ghosts from
the dark wood.

II.

Down the tracks, valleys
are still frontiers, barren
farms break hands tilling
fumble fingers tumbling.

There are specters, spooks
in dead mine nooks of empty
burial mounds - a curse reversed

by holy reverie guru whispers
snake oil slogans like cure all
candle elixir protection -

cannot stop murder curse
in hotels and poisoned wells
wish for a parlor trickster.

Dead crops are omens, so
fathers paint barns red with
hex Dutch magic when
the good book fails.

We are children at the train stop,
waiting for what the city spilled
sinful down rail lines, listening
for a steam whistle down
the dark tunnel.

Dry

Sleep frayed as doll spun in dust devil,
    threads fail to hold

bile in the pit when pills do not bite,
    vile venom spits

muted moon-lit jet trails,
    umbilical.

Reborn into night, yoke of pollen angst,
    moth dust blinks angels

in rusted window screens incandescent
    porch-lit incubator.

Mumble in tongues, forgotten incantation
    of sleep unsoundly,

a fox glides past an aging oak,
    sways godmother arms.

Vines sprawl across rooftops, a microsound
    of worms winding

winding over mortar and stone,
    compost of chrysalis.

How It Ends

I. Split

Someday you will split
from my fitful fear,
spawned from
organ pits spilling
silent sinew,
terminal.

You have waited,
a sleeping beast,
you are awake;
grown from
guttural patience,
pit of pestilence.

II. Clot.

Patient as a spider
poised to pounce,
venom to ventricle;
you will strike,
between a blink
of lashes leaping,
during sleep's web
or wakeful step
or weary thrust,

you will crawl
itsy bitsy up the
waterspout.

III. Last

At the final hour, she chants
canticles for confession.

I can taste the censer
kiss through locked
gates collapsing;
your rusted tongue,
a draw-bridge
unraveling.

When I take
my last breath,
neither the taste of
your poison mouth
nor lithium litanies
will shake my chest,
or take me home.

IV. Ash

Father, I do not want
to be a shroud to
crowd your sleep.

I do not want
to disturb your dirt,
shift your stone.

I want to be
ash dashed around
your bones.

I am not worth
the wake of your vault,
to lie by your side.

I am resolved
to weeds in winter,
soil in summer.

Peeling

We are
   left-handed pathfinders
peeling
forth formed
for solitude
from the froth
of mongrel.

We are
   anti this that anti
art
raging allegory
the poet
   must present
resets, reeling -

seven
signs selective
seven
seas electric
seven.

Drown

My manifest destiny
is a car crash memory
into river Lethe to wash

blood and sand of
my shrapnel-burned
friends buried below

stones on the shore;
tourists swarm silent,
so I dive into the deep

coffin of cobblestones
where I never swim
where I can sleep

a dreamless sacrifice to
never remember to
never remember again.

Geography in Ether

There is a geography
that exists in every

dream, I know each
path - a winding trail

of forest behind the old
house I never lived in.

The grid of an unreal
city that has never existed,

know where to hide when
tides break and bombs fall.

I would know where
to go - if eyes were open.

Some believe memories
can be passed through

DNA strands, programmed,
and wonder where blood

takes me, if memories of
dreams collide in code.

Full of Noise

My head is full of noise,
reverberate in white cotton,
so it does not spill, from ears.

Tongue prevents a song
from stomach bellowing
forth harmonium carbonate

eyes register skull husk
howl when hounds summon
the night in dreams.

I am full of noise, as a hive
ringing insect drone -
I am the drone.

Wake

The aquamarine print over
your bed radiates a submerged
slumber dirge as you sleep.

From your lips' lunar incantation,
sutras rise as air bubble dreams
to Hecate's night-broken swim;

I am suspended as a boy
under linen waiting for sunlight
to bleed through blinds to wake.

We wake for Shiva in a shanty
where everything is sacred -
the bruised sky after rain.

We wake for moth mothers
missing altars of allegory,
collapsing under optic ash.

We wake for the goddess
caught in city fountains,
bathing in halogen halos.

Five

At five, the fallout shelter
meant nothing, five miles
from Pentagon ground zero.

Five sides to a graveyard,
five emergency broadcast
beeps, squelching forth;

the large yellow iron siren
outside the playground was
not a tornado siren – it bellows
before missiles fall.

Five places to hide:

    Five
Under the basement stairs
coiled under carpenter nails,
a splintered coffin for plastic
action figures, melts a mold
for toy guns, discharge sparks.

    Four
Deep into the storm drains
until fire passed flesh, expels
family from concrete canals
a radiation birth.

   Three
In dreams I cannot wake
to burn, a human candle
of fat and hair smoldering;
it is never better to
duck and cover.

   Two
If Father could drive past
mountains, a survivor in
a Monday night mini-series,
mothers embrace children
turn to nature in ashes
-in ashes.

   One
The sky will fall – there is no
fifth horse to flee from fire –
we all hide in Mother's arms
-we all fall down.

Wake the Goddess

I could go to church if
a goddess was on the altar;
no war conversion, but
a kiss to sleep under her
starry umbra, dark matter
binding dreams as broken
limbs in the nursery.

No more "He died
For Our Sins" so we
pray in lamentation;

she slept as sin, so
she should always be
awake in supplication.

Mother madrigal matins,
so there is no Satan to
shelter us in homes
as strays -

this is the way we sing

this is how we kill the king.

Land of the Blind

We are legion in a
leper's march, leagues
to Lazarus - a lost

minute march, goose
step minuet, singing
loose before a minaret.

Pennants blaze Charon's
spent chevrons, we dance
in a blind broadcast.

Quicksilver is seething,
siphoned in silence - a
slip of our tinsel tongues;

We will tie tourniquets,
quills to paper, arrows
to quiver, to fell fear.

But we die on the streets,
staccato of bullets, brass;
brass horns blow a dirge,

we shatter like safety glass -
we die on the streets, waltz
of mid-west symphonies.

There is a northern wind,
white light of winter; I hope
it bends, bites paper kites

that cut, that kill - downs
paper towers, burns paper
power in the howl of love.

Train Stop

There was magic waiting
for the train with Father;
tossing grey gravel across
tracks, staring for hours
at summer's humid
horizon glaze, hopeful.

Listening through a drone
of cicadas and crickets
for the bell, the long
stripped arms fell and
black metal light posts
blinked red, a wink to
acknowledge the secret
of steel and timing.

When the engine passed,
the conductor waved, so
I pulled my arms down,
as gesture to whistle.

Some Kind of Mass

Mother made capes,
paper plate masks with
magic markers.

Father forged an ink
stamp fan club letter
for a five year old.

I was forged from
Saturday morning
heroes saving mankind

in a half hour turn we
are mild-mannered,
Captain Marvelous.

Mother sewed merit
badges on official
scout boys bound

in colored scarves,
as a noodle necklace
noose singing holy

rosary safety patrol
saint Mary, an after
school 38 special.

Busy busy work
fathers bound from
metro buses after five,

brass buttons on olive
uniforms blossom
achtung action figures,

posable but praying
for playboys with
grape juice grins,

graceful as a "Blessed
Be" bishop bumper
sticker confirmation.

I was never saved.
Dead deacons dry
on my doorstep.

Tasks

If I could place you
behind plastic sheets,
dust of your polaroid

finish shrine, then the
spine of spiral rings
could hold all these

things as yellowed-prints
caught in album adhesive,
breathing ardor of aging,

an adoration of family,
so we could light incense
to adore a fugue state's

mask when we flip pages -
a task of offspring.

Painted Saints

Cathedrals are often silent;
pre-recorded monastic murmurs
creep into corners, a soundtrack
to tennis shoes screeching past
photo shutter clacks in sepia.

This cathedral is different;
at night, on rain-stained stone
a warm glow of Byzantine red
under a bell tower balcony
reflects blood candles on
refectory doors.

Behind Zaborovsky gate,
censer smoke dissipates;
painted saints fade on
warped wooden frescos,
as apparitions fade.

I could light a candle
for pilgrim or pillage
if I smoked, or prayed;

instead, I will burn
a plastic doll,
Our Lady Mary
Matryoshka.

Stage Two

Royal discharge for
wounded cavalry
dashing standard issue
flash sale 9.99
99 bullets excised
99 child soldiers hushed

   running...
marble carriage canopy
reeling film running
nowhere cranes
   in reverse...

A lens burns misanthropes -
tournament of internment
moths pinned to sonnet
tears searing pineal iris

   gazing...
glandular soul, third eye,
seeping serotonin phosphorus
burns photoreceptors
   in reverse...

bioluminescent beetles
break coffins - balance
together on tainted
fiber optics, tight-wired
necrotic sinew

breathing...
an empress disdained droll
doll fetish drone technique,
suitors unfold in spring
jinx-worn corsets, juxtaposed
    in reverse....

Fear of Gold

Wretched poison mouth
spills god spittle,

cursed coins and collars
cough under leagues,

laugh and scoff under
salt tide umbra.

Royal luster licks saint locks,
coiled serpent chains

scald skin silent;
a regal blood banner

beckons bones with
blade or bullet.

Immaculate sheen of lust
sweat-bit rock chasm chisels,

swings like the long hand
lapping rusted stars.

Sickle Moon

The sickle moon rose,
ate lotus petals sick

as rose light locked
in a fickle loon song,

licked a wound by
a frozen lake, fed

a wandering hare far
in the wear of winter.

Fox stares into wood,
hunted by feral stars

under moonlight,
a haunted dance.

The hungry wind
shakes husks on

swaying boughs,
death rattle of a

dying man's secret.
You cannot run

from rain marching
across leaves, faint

as static whispers
- a dead channel.

District

From five thousand feet
you are not a real city
but foliage and concrete;

a parade of Grecian ghosts
march in peppered plastic
patchwork, grafted with glass.

Weary wasteland of marble
murder markups, you are made
from syringe and soapbox.

You do not have a tongue,
you have a rasping cough,
tour bus engine cacophony;

if you did, you could taste
vermin kill of metro rail
brakes and stale monuments.

You are not a real city,
but I am still stuck to your
August asphalt adhesive.

Paint the Stars

Without water, a bruised
tumble down the slide

turns to stop in hope's
barren harvest cutting;

I cannot paint the boy
unformed, but carve

tiny scars on canvas,
no promise of limbs.

He plays at night,
crawls with a plastic

rifle through broken
limbs in the backyard,

he has lost pinned laurels
and medals, arrested in

pine needles under a
cloud-stricken moon.

Watch him eat a pastry
on a cafe chair, he stares

at light sockets until the sky
is grey without clouds,

nothing to leave but words
in a wake, paint on a wall.

Pillbox is an empty vessel, no
longer aware of breath,

landmarks are meaningless
in a forest of houses when

we need the ocean's empty
edge of night, tides change

the volume in chests, influx of
breath under a speckled-worn

canopy of stars; we are planted
in sand to wait.

Spent stars fall to find graves,
seed with murmur and song,

reeds of bones rattle to sing in
electric tongues past rain-rust

radio tower spines painted red
 - so I paint the stars.

Kiss the glass kindly as a
fable-bent farewell, I want it

to be real, on empty canvas;
shells and peels of skin litter

sleep with apathy
 - so I paint the stars.

Sleeping Alone

Drink me to sleep,
framed with marionette
architecture of Mary;
hopeless on strings,

grin of nicotine-stained
jaundice jowls.

Spring-heeled whispers,
whiskey-spouted when
stars shake fists at
my white whiskers,
shrunken head.

Drink me to sleep,
to silence forty years,
learning to forget.

We can be beasts
to bellow, my fellow.

Rewind

No one is ever from here.
Yet, I was spawned from
cicada husks on bark,
sparkler smoke,
yoke of wet asphalt,
fear of fallout.

I am native to sidewalks,
with a fear of slashers;
where stars disappear,
where marching band
drums carry a dirge
caught in cul-de-sacs.

We hid in storm drains,
dreamed of the bomb,
a Friday night film
retracted, on fire.

The Groundskeepers

Today will always be your birthday;
when I can no longer lay flowers,
today will still be your birthday.

Today you would want icing
and so many words, but
sugar would melt in grass –

groundskeepers would take the cards.

Today you would want flowers;
I could plant seeds, let July
rains raise a floral blanket –

groundskeepers would cut them down.

Today you would want to run;
rising to race against yourself
down winding asphalt paths –

groundskeepers would push you down.

The Wick

The torque of a dervish dance,
a palm at zenith in supplication,
alms to ego death like celestial
bodies spin, an invisible axis;

yet I am drawn into the floor,
foot to grave displaced by
gravity into Demeter's earth
as the good godson should.

      Looking for rhythm and meter
      taping aging toes in socks
      as I could…

I tell myself, there is no use
no faithful fulcrum winds,
from a fitful fuse, an unlit
muse, the wick of the unkind.

Concussion

In the smoke of a car crash
airbag burns my face;
the stereo is too loud
song still playing
louder than sirens.

We are glass vessels to spill
currents as memory effluence
when we walk in circles –
water through cracks.

Opaque glass, what is outside?
The bone shell of DNA where
water stains our walk.

Stowaway

Little boy bedrooms are blue,
blankets covered in clipper
ships and steering wheels,

grandfathers who have never sailed
wear nautical-themed aftershave
as false sea captains.

Ocean is a mother I could not
conquest with mast and cannon –
we are insignificant at night.

Shivering

When you no longer drink,
toasts are meaningless,
winter cuts bone;

you are truly alone
when forms defined
as broken husks of

locust shells, perched
on high chairs sing
from door drafts.

The howl of kinship
offerings now shake
the night in dance.

This was how I could sing -
now a thief with an
empty cup, shivering.

Tolls

Because a dust particle passing
the optic lens drifts in your
periphery, sleeps in orbit.

Have not used eye before
because of Imagists
because eye was never
important, discarded

as torn tissue, or
worn skin disposed
a wakeful juxtapose
begins to take
a toll, because.

Dry

Sleep frayed as doll spun in dust devil,
    threads fail to hold
bile in the pit when pills do not bite,
    vile venom spits
muted moon-lit jet trails,
    umbilical.
Reborn into night, yoke of pollen angst,
    moth dust blinks angels
in rusted window screens incandescent,
    porch-lit incubator.
Mumble in tongues, forgotten incantation
    of sleep unsoundly,
a fox glides past an aging oak,
    sways godmother arms.
Vines sprawl across rooftops, a microsound
    of worms winding
winding over mortar and stone,
    compost of chrysalis.

Everything is Just Fine

Radio plays pop requiems on
the long commute home;
perfect pitch dance steps,
        everything is just fine.

To make us forget
the world is on fire
we pretend not to choke
on smoke of cinders
from embryo to embers
smoldering pop up screens
is a warning broadcast,
        everything is just fine.

My eyes bleed with each
channel switched – wipe
the itch, wipe them clean,
        everything is just fine.

Children die in the street
bullets replayed, streaming
so we will not burn in
high-definition sugar kilns,
in figments of distraction
or fragments of distinction,
but in a rain-rusted radio
hiss of static bliss believing
        everything is just fine.

The Fog

You do not know who
I am when I call your room.
Yesterday I asked father
at his grave in hopes that
on his birthday he would
listen carefully, past a
flower veneration offering –

to find you in the mist
as I believe spirits could,
dancing between
blood marker distance
in a vast, dark wood.

Perhaps he could convince
you to wake – perhaps
you would listen.

Last night I prayed –
a first time in years
for a miracle tether

to lull you out of fog,
to lure you past wires,
past the squelch of
twilight – into the white
of open arms.

Cult of Self

Catalog and collect;
because I cannot hope
to kiss sheen from
screen glow soft –
it means nothing.

Self-exile self-exhume
selfish flash self-help sale
ultra self to flesh ourselves –
I am nothing.

So this is where we are;
rebrand reborn rebirth
the pixel flare fails to
fall in strands of ocean
light as we are clicking
we are clicking
we are clicking
nothing.

For Lovers

I.

Through windows of an evening
commute, bureaucrats explode
under starched collars as a dying
star martyred in the weltschmerz
of a humid hatchback.

We are all watching breaking news from
nursing home windows, chair-bound
hands in fist shaking helpless when
bridges collapse, corpses burn,
parking lots empty.

II.

Karate moms count coupons from
shopping cart battle rams, berating
stock duty Sikhs under breath;
this land is my land
this land's not your land
I am your landlady
do not shake my hand
in fist.

Anger will spill upon asphalt
with 9 millimeters and many calibers
from iron-forged calipers and calcium
supplements calibrating ranged weapon
hands waving higher for high capacity,
high definition – without fidelity.

Wave goodbye to horizons bent to humid
highways for some heaven up there,
somewhere angels will gather exploded
stars in a paper bag of angst – light it
and leave it on a doorstep - a child's
ice cream melts – spills upon dirt.

Anthems (for a Generation)

Pixelated dreams scratch
broken long hands,
saturate the bone

pacified by anxiety pills
scream soft white –
but only a whisper.

Televised or posted
in sepia profile
popularity contest;

Select consumer pick
prophet code fame
routing compressed.

Select consumer sick
stroboscopic flash in
an empty room.

Select consumer cut
to feel and bleed to
prove – we are real.

Walk through windows
faster than walls
decay with poison

in a data dream,
the grey taste of
mourning streamed.

Resort Photograph

American Standard,
urinal font for foxtrot,
you tap dance for falconry
the trap of ivy balcony,
a spine of brick ballet.

A gallery of resort photos hang
in the water closet, faded men
grin with hollow faces, washed
pale in mineral springs -
ghosts under glass.

Bravado of talking boards
tonic of walking herds
distant bells ring past
a green briar glen –
lure of liar's lips.

Hymnals and hyacinth,
braided girls parade
past pulpits, track
pasture to tombstone.

Parasols and parapets,
silent eyes pose under
molding, where mortar
could hide murder.

Standing on green tile,
I could be a memory
in splintered filter, a
weary form, dancing.

Monster

As long as children
can play alone
on the sidewalk -
carve chalk cranes on
cement steps without
fear, we will thrive;
        I grow weary, yet
        still cannot sleep -
        I cannot father.

As long as children
can dream alone
lulled into sleep,
dispel monster forms
to care for strangers,
we will thrive;
        my limbs are numb
        from fighting –
        I cannot dream.

Torchlight

Pull me from despair
of blankets with torchlit
thresholds under stars.

Doors are open to pines,
swaying power lines pulse
without the moon.

Wandering blind to keys
opening each footstep on
the frigid lawn to skin.

A dog barks down the path,
wrath of a crossroads – so
I cannot look back.

You in Delphi

As an oracle would read my liver
as a lover could unbind me,
deliver the ocean to lips.

You dissect me with wisps
of unrested whispers,
trail of silk tresses.

And I am numb today
and all has lost its luster
without the drink of

strangers in the dark
behind denim longing
to pierce skin – as ink.

www.ingramcontent.com/pod-product-compliance
Lightning Source LLC
Chambersburg PA
CBHW032134090426
42743CB00007B/589